SEVEN MYSTERY MELODIES

ROUNDS FOR LIKE STRING INSTRUMENTS OR STRING ORCHESTRA

BY MATTHEW HOEY

This creative collection presents seven original rounds, each written from the scrambled notes of a traditional tune. Play these entertaining pieces through from the beginning like traditional rounds. When all four parts of each round are played together, the well-known melody of its related tune appears. To identify the mystery melody, listen to the entire group as they play. Though the mystery melody cannot be identified in the individual parts, at the end of each round, an "Unscrambled Ensemble" version can help solve the mystery. Try swapping parts in this section.

Throughout this book, courtesy accidentals are used to help you learn correct finger patterns. These markings, along with some bowing patterns, are only marked in their initial appearance. Future appearances are generally not marked to encourage you to remember how to perform them as part of your musical development.

The pieces may be performed with only four cellos, or with as many as you like—just split up into four groups. The string basses may perform the accompaniment parts on the "Mystery Melody" pages as the cellos perform the round. The bass parts beginning on page 24 include the melody and can be played as a bass ensemble by two, three, or four basses (or more!). You can swap parts and take turns playing the melodies.

There's also a matching book for violins and violas, so you can play with them, too—when you play the melody, they play a special ensemble accompaniment. And when they play the melody, you can use the accompaniment parts in this book. Your teacher can also play the piano accompaniments that are provided in the teacher's score.

Have fun!

Matthew Hoey

CONTENTS

Alfred Music
P.O. Box 10003
Van Nuys, CA 91410-0003
alfred.com

ISBN-10: 1-4706-4355-3
ISBN-13: 978-1-4706-4355-3

Cover author photo courtesy of Matthew Hoey
Additional art resources courtesy of Getty Images

1. SO SHE ONLY MADE ONE SWEATER

Mystery Melody

Play the scrambled tune as a traditional round. Your teacher will divide the Cello players into four groups. The first group should begin the round by playing through part I and moving to part II when finished, continuing this way through parts III and IV and then back to part I. The second group should start part I eight measures after the first group and continue through the other parts as well. The next two groups should play the parts in the same manner, beginning eight measures after the preceding group. *Parts should finish __together__, meaning that some players will not be at the end of the page when the piece ends*. The round can be repeated as many times as desired.

CELLO

1. SO SHE ONLY MADE ONE SWEATER

Unscrambled Ensemble

Play the unscrambled ensemble four times, and switch parts on each repeat.

What is the name of this tune? _____

Accompaniment

If you're playing the tune as a string orchestra, use the following accompaniment when the Violins and Violas have the melody. Repeat as directed by the teacher.

2. IT'S EASIER THAN SWIMMING

Mystery Melody

Play the scrambled tune as a traditional round. Your teacher will divide the Cello players into four groups. The first group should begin the round by playing through part I and moving to part II when finished, continuing this way through parts III and IV and then back to part I. The second group should start part I sixteen measures after the first group and continue through the other parts as well. The next two groups should play the parts in the same manner, beginning sixteen measures after the preceding group. *Parts should finish together, meaning that some players will not be at the end of the page when the piece ends.* The round can be repeated as many times as desired.

CELLO

2. IT'S EASIER THAN SWIMMING

Unscrambled Ensemble

Play the unscrambled ensemble four times, and switch parts on each repeat.

What is the name of this tune? _____

CELLO

Accompaniment

If you're playing the tune as a string orchestra, use the following accompaniment when the Violins and Violas have the melody. Repeat as directed by the teacher.

3. IN APRIL

Mystery Melody

Play the scrambled tune as a traditional round. Your teacher will divide the Cello players into four groups. The first group should begin the round by playing through part I and moving to part II when finished, continuing this way through parts III and IV and then back to part I. The second group should start part I fourteen measures after the first group and continue through the other parts as well. The next two groups should play the parts in the same manner, beginning fourteen measures after the preceding group. *Parts should finish together, meaning that some players will not be at the end of the page when the piece ends.* The round can be repeated as many times as desired.

CELLO

III.

IV.

3. IN APRIL

Unscrambled Ensemble

Play the unscrambled ensemble four times, and switch parts on each repeat.

What is the name of this tune? _____

Accompaniment

If you're playing the tune as a string orchestra, use the following accompaniment when the Violins and Violas have the melody. Repeat as directed by the teacher.

4. SHINY!

Mystery Melody

Play the scrambled tune as a traditional round. Your teacher will divide the Cello players into four groups. The first group should begin the round by playing through part I and moving to part II when finished, continuing this way through parts III and IV and then back to part I. The second group should start part I twelve measures after the first group and continue through the other parts as well. The next two groups should play the parts in the same manner, beginning twelve measures after the preceding group. *Parts should finish* *together*, *meaning that some players will not be at the end of the page when the piece ends*. The round can be repeated as many times as desired.

CELLO

4. SHINY!

Unscrambled Ensemble

Play the unscrambled ensemble four times, and switch parts on each repeat.

What is the name of this tune? _____

Accompaniment

If you're playing the tune as a string orchestra, use the following accompaniment when the Violins and Violas have the melody. Repeat as directed by the teacher.

5. IT WAS ONLY A MODEL

Mystery Melody

Play the scrambled tune as a traditional round. Your teacher will divide the Cello players into four groups. The first group should begin the round by playing through part I and moving to part II when finished, continuing this way through parts III and IV and then back to part I. The second group should start part I sixteen measures after the first group and continue through the other parts as well. The next two groups should play the parts in the same manner, beginning sixteen measures after the preceding group. *Parts should finish <u>together</u>, meaning that some players will not be at the end of the page when the piece ends.* The round can be repeated as many times as desired.

III.

IV.

5. IT WAS ONLY A MODEL

Unscrambled Ensemble

Play the unscrambled ensemble four times, and switch parts on each repeat.

What is the name of this tune? _____

CELLO

Accompaniment

If you're playing the tune as a string orchestra, use the following accompaniment when the Violins and Violas have the melody. Repeat as directed by the teacher.

6. SURPRISE!

Mystery Melody

Play the scrambled tune as a traditional round. Your teacher will divide the Cello players into four groups. The first group should begin the round by playing through part I and moving to part II when finished, continuing this way through parts III and IV and then back to part I. The second group should start part I sixteen measures after the first group and continue through the other parts as well. The next two groups should play the parts in the same manner, beginning sixteen measures after the preceding group. *Parts should finish together, meaning that some players will not be at the end of the page when the piece ends.* The round can be repeated as many times as desired.

CELLO

III.

IV.

6. SURPRISE!

Unscrambled Ensemble

Play the unscrambled ensemble four times, and switch parts on each repeat.

What is the name of this tune? _____

CELLO

Accompaniment

If you're playing the tune as a string orchestra, use the following accompaniment when the Violins and Violas have the melody. Repeat as directed by the teacher.

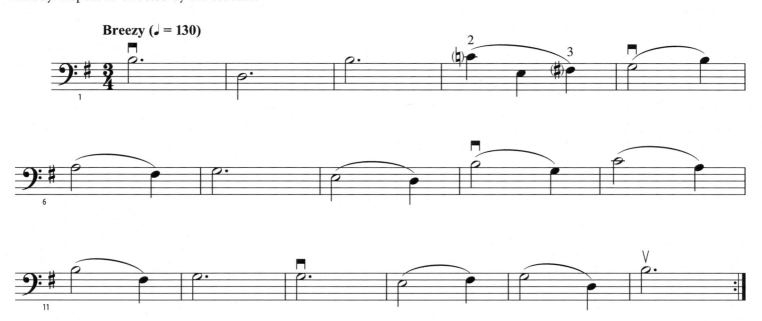

7. BAZ TEALE

Mystery Melody

Play the scrambled tune as a traditional round. Your teacher will divide the Cello players into four groups. The first group should begin the round by playing through part I and moving to part II when finished, continuing this way through parts III and IV and then back to part I. The second group should start part I eight measures after the first group and continue through the other parts as well. The next two groups should play the parts in the same manner, beginning eight measures after the preceding group. *Parts should finish <u>together</u>, meaning that some players will not be at the end of the page when the piece ends.* The round can be repeated as many times as desired.

7. BAZ TEALE

Unscrambled Ensemble

Play the unscrambled ensemble four times, and switch parts on each repeat.

What is the name of this tune? _____

Accompaniment

If you're playing the tune as a string orchestra, use the following accompaniment when the Violins and Violas have the melody. Repeat as directed by the teacher.

1. SO SHE ONLY MADE ONE SWEATER

Unscrambled String Bass Ensemble

When the Cellos have the tune, use line I, II, or III. You can switch parts on each repeat.

What is the name of this tune? _____

Accompaniment

When playing as a string orchestra, use the following accompaniment when the Violins and Violas have the tune. Repeat as directed by the teacher.

STRING BASS

2. IT'S EASIER THAN SWIMMING

Unscrambled String Bass Ensemble

When the Cellos have the tune, use line I, II, or III. You can switch parts on each repeat.

What is the name of this tune? _____

Accompaniment

If you're playing the tune as a string orchestra, use the following accompaniment when the Violins and Violas have the melody. Repeat as directed by the teacher.

STRING BASS

3. IN APRIL

Unscrambled String Bass Ensemble

When the Cellos have the tune, use line I, II, or III. You can switch parts on each repeat.

What is the name of this tune? _____

† Play the cue notes when a String Bass is playing the melody.

Accompaniment

If you're playing the tune as a string orchestra, use the following accompaniment when the Violins and Violas have the melody. Repeat as directed by the teacher.

STRING BASS

4. SHINY!

Unscrambled String Bass Ensemble

When the Cellos have the tune, use line I, II, or III. You can switch parts on each repeat.

What is the name of this tune? _____

Accompaniment

If you're playing the tune as a string orchestra, use the following accompaniment when the Violins and Violas have the melody. Repeat as directed by the teacher.

5. IT WAS ONLY A MODEL

Unscrambled String Bass Ensemble

When the Cellos have the tune, use line I, II, or III. You can switch parts on each repeat.

What is the name of this tune? _____

† Play the cue notes when a String Bass is playing the melody.

Accompaniment

When playing as a string orchestra, use the following accompaniment when the Violins and Violas have the tune. Repeat as directed by the teacher.

6. SURPRISE!

Unscrambled String Bass Ensemble

When the Cellos have the tune, use line I, II, or III. You can switch parts on each repeat.

What is the name of this tune? _____

STRING BASS

Accompaniment

When playing as a string orchestra, use the following accompaniment when the Violins and Violas have the tune. Repeat as directed by the teacher.

7. BAZ TEALE

Unscrambled String Bass Ensemble

When the Cellos have the tune, use line I, II, or III. You can switch parts on each repeat.

What is the name of this tune? _____

† Play the cue notes when a String Bass is playing the melody.

Accompaniment

When playing as a string orchestra, use the following accompaniment when the Violins and Violas have the tune. Repeat as directed by the teacher.